# Lochleven's Royal Prisoner

## Mary Queen of Scots

by

Nancy H. Walker

© 1983

Published by Mrs. N. H. Walker
2 Muirpark Road, Kinross

Printed by Woods of Perth (Printers) Ltd.
3-5 Mill Street, Perth

# THANKS

The author wishes to thank many friends who helped in the preparation of this book.  Among these were :

The Reference Department of the Sandeman Library in Perth.
Mr Nigel Tranter, novelist, Mr Duncan McNaughton, F.S.A.Scot. and Mr David M Munro, F.S.A.Scot., who advised and encouraged.
Mr Andrew Thorburn D.A., pupils and staff of Kinross High School Art Department, and others who helped to illustrate the pages.

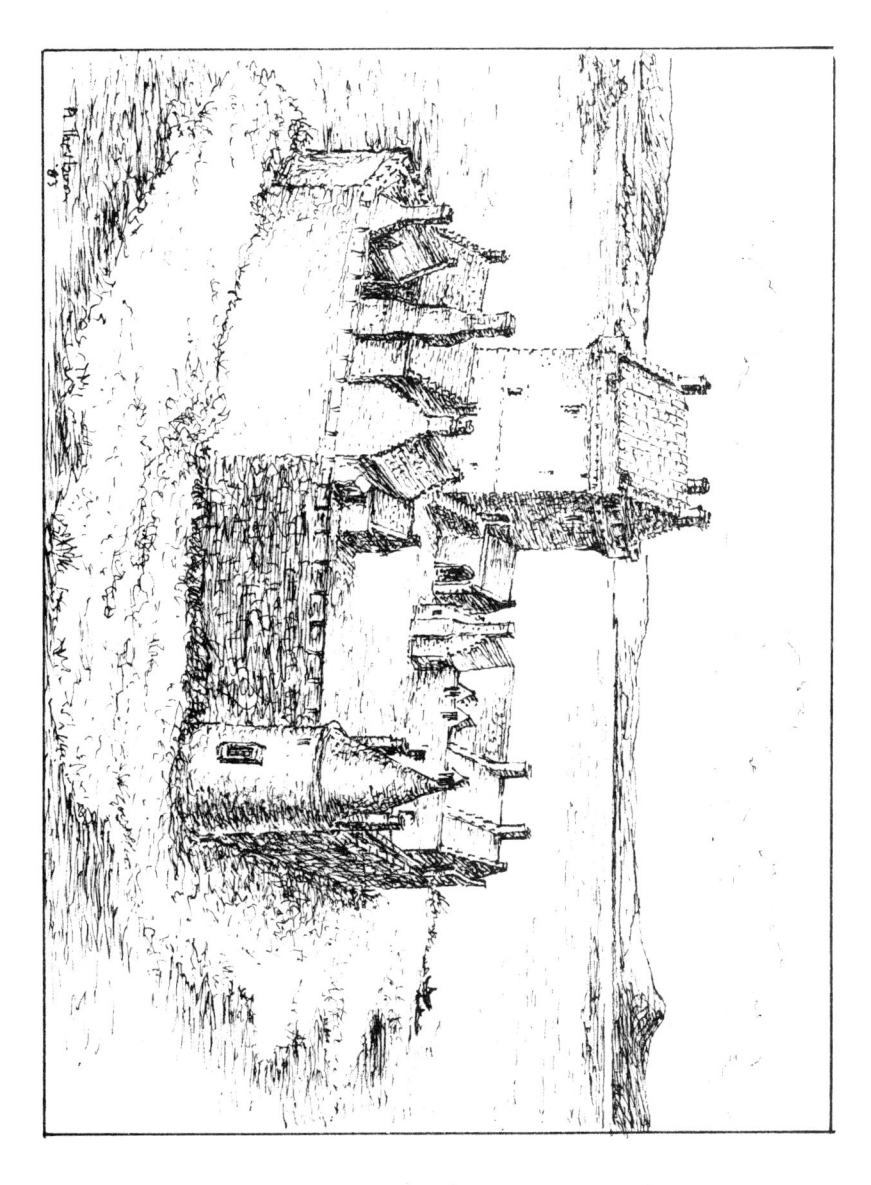

*LOCH LEVEN CASTLE (RECONSTRUCTION)*
By ANDREW THORBURN D.A.
Adapted from John Begg (1897)

## ILLUSTRATIONS

*COVER MONTAGE by ANDREW THORBURN and SHONA E. KINNAIRD*

|  |  | page |
|---|---|---|
| Lochleven Castle | Andrew Thorburn | iii |
| Mr Robert Burns-Begg | Brian Rowley | v |
| Elevation of the Tower Keep | Andrew Thorburn | 7 |
| Ground Plan of the Castle | John Begg (Adapted) | 9 |
| Thistle, Rose and Fleur de Lis | Mandy Webster | 15 |
| John Knox | anon. | 20 |
| The Earl of Bothwell | Annan (S.N.P.G.) | 24 |
| The Castle in the Loch | John Begg | 26 |
| The Earl of Moray | Annan (S.N.P.G.) | 32 |
| The Abdication | anon. | 35 |
| Queen Mary in her Room | John Begg | 39 |
| The Queen in Disguise | Pauline E. Brown | 41 |
| The Postern Gate | anon. (Antiquarians) | 47 |
| Mary After Years of Captivity | Pauline E. Brown | 52 |
| The Executioner | Shona E. Kinnaird | 56 |
| The Castle as it is Now | Irene Aitken | 57 |

## CONTENTS

|  |  | page |
|---|---|---|
| Foreword |  | 1 |
| Chapter 1 : | Lochleven Castle | 2 |
| 2 : | The Castle as Queen Mary Knew It | 8 |
| 3 : | Events Leading to Mary's Imprisonment | 13 |
| 4 : | Mary's Second and Third Marriages | 21 |
| 5 : | The Royal Prisoner | 27 |
| 6 : | The Abdication | 31 |
| 7 : | A Wearisome Time | 36 |
| 8 : | The Rescue | 43 |
| 9 : | Trapped in England | 51 |
| Reading List |  | 57 |

Mr. ROBERT BURNS-BEGG F.S.A. Scot.
*1823-1897*
*Kinross historian, to whom this book is dedicated.*

(Photo by Brian Rowley)

# FOREWORD

Mary Stewart, or Stuart (the French version of her name, which she preferred) was either hated or loved by those who knew her. There were no half measures.

She must have been a fascinating person of great charm and dignity, a woman born to be Queen, and endowed with fortitude and strength of character to face up to the most terrifying and painful experiences. No-one could have led a more tragic life.

Many of the Queen's troubles were due to bad luck, while others arose from her impetuous nature and lack of judgment. But the most bitter of her troubles were caused by people who, for one reason or another, were determined that Mary would not remain on the throne of Scotland.

So many biographies of Mary Stuart have already been produced that this little book needs only to outline briefly the events which led to her imprisonment in Lochleven Castle, and the years following her escape. The central part of this account deals in more detail with her imprisonment on the island from 17th June 1567 to the 2nd May 1568, eleven months which are usually mentioned only briefly by historians, but are of particular interest to the people of Kinross and visitors to the Castle. The subject of her escape has always been of romantic speculation and legend.

Much detailed information about this period has been provided by Mr Robert Burns-Begg, a much-respected local historian who in 1887 published a book entitled "The History of Lochleven Castle". He later revised and renamed the book "The Secrets of My Prison House". It was published a few months after his death, in 1901. The author had a long, close connection with both Loch and Castle, and was very interested in the "tragic experiences of its fairest martyr".

Unfortunately, both books are out of print, so his knowledge, together with the results of additional research, are here published for those who are interested in Lochleven's royal prisoner.

# CHAPTER 1

## LOCHLEVEN CASTLE

### In Days of Yore

Imagine, if you can, the days of long ago when the level of Loch Leven was 4½ feet, or nearly 1½ metres, higher than it is now, and the Castle Island was therefore a good deal smaller. There was probably a primitive fortress on it as far back as the days of the Picts but, of course, there is nothing of that to be seen now. The early history of the Castle is "hidden in the mists of time", but Mr Burns-Begg tells us that in 1256 the boy-king, Alexander 111 and his even younger Queen ( a daughter of Henry 111 of England ) were taken from what must have been an earlier castle on the island, and carried off to Stirling to be kept safe from the English invaders.

### Wallace Wins the Island

In the first half of the 17th century, Sir James Balfour of Kinnaird made a collection of manuscripts which he named "Annals and Short Passages of State". These were published in 1884. According to Sir James, the island in Loch Leven was besieged by the English in 1301, but was quickly retaken by Sir John Comyn. In October 1303 Edward 1's army was in Dunfermline resting up for the winter, when Sir William Wallace, who had severely defeated a superior English force at Stirling Bridge in 1297, carried out a daring exploit. This is recounted in "The Lay of Blind Harry, the Minstrel", dated about 1470. In Mr Burns-Begg's modernised paraphrase of the "Homeric effusion" the Minstrel relates that:

> The Scots at large over-ran all Fife,
> And of the Englishmen none were left in that country.
> But in Lochleven there lay a company upon that Inch,
> In a small house they had prepared  -
> Castle was none, but surrounded by water 'wicht'.

Wallace made a rendezvous with a knight called Grey at Scotland Well, where they settled for the night. After supper, Wallace took eighteen of his men to attack the "Royal hold". The next part of the account is somewhat confusing, but seems to claim that Wallace himself swam naked to St Serf's Island, where he collected a boat, then he and his men rowed to the other island and attacked the garrison:

> *The Island they took, drawn sword in hand,*
> *And spared none that they found before them;*
> *Struck doors up, and stabbed men where they lay.*
> *Upon the Southerns thus sadly did they rush;*
> *Thirty they slew that were in that place.*
> *Their five women Wallace sent off that 'sted'.*
> *Woman nor bairn he never caused put to death.*

Wallace then sent for his other men to join them on the island, and they had a fine feast of all the Englishmen's rations, before moving on to St Johnstoun ( Perth )

In 1335 Lochleven Castle was being held on behalf of the Scottish King David 11 by Sir Allan Vipon, or Vipont, when it was besieged by Sir John Stryvelyne ( Stirling ) "a renegade Scotsman", helped by English soldiers. In what is now the Kirkgate Cemetery they built a fort of earth and turf, as a base from which to attack the Castle. However, the garrison on the island not only repelled the attackers, but also attacked the fort and killed many men, so Stryvelyne was forced to call off the siege.

**A Royal Castle**

In 1328 Lochleven was listed as one of the Royal Castles, others being Edinburgh, Stirling and Dumbarton; King David 11 gave orders for them all to be prepared to resist enemy attacks by Edward 111 of England (This must surely be the castle we now see on the island, for it was built in the 14th century) But after Edward Baliol, backed by Edward, had invaded Scotland in 1332, Lochleven was mentioned as one of only four castles remaining in King David's hands; the others were Urquhart, Kildrummie and Dumbarton. However, by 1341 the English had been driven out of all the Scottish strongholds.

The simple, high tower was the only building on the island for about 200 years, until the early 16th century, when the other buildings and the high ramparts, or curtain walls, round the courtyard were added. There was also an elevated walkway round the inside of the parapet, from which the sentinels could keep watch in all directions over the Loch. Outside the rampart wall there would probably be some smaller buildings of wood or stone, such as a bakery and fuel stores. There was a small garden to the north of the tower, but there was space for little else. If there were, as now, two landing-stages, they would be nearer the castle, and the rampart walls would rise almost directly from the water's edge.

**The Tower**

The Castle itself is really a "Tower Keep", a type of fortified home common in Scotland in the troubled 16th century. There are several similar tower-houses in Kinross-shire, such as Cleish Castle and Burleigh Castle, but Lochleven was one of the Royal Castles used by the monarchs not only in times of war but also, like Falkland Palace, as hunting-lodges in times of peace.

A pamphlet published by the Department of the Environment has been of great assistance in dealing with the archaeology of the buildings, but Mr Burns-Begg was able to study these over 100 years ago, when they were in a much better state preservation, so his comments are also very helpful.

The tower is oblong in shape, and originally had five storeys including a kind of pent-house under the steep roof; both have now disappeared. The upper windows of the tower used to have external shutters, for protection from weather or enemy action. The south-east corner rises square right up to the top, and inside this corner there is a circular stairway. On top of the other three corners there are open rounds whose lower parts are solid drums of masonry.

**The Entrance**

Originally the only way into the Castle was through the arched doorway high up in the east wall on the second storey, so that

- 4 -

the Castle could be easily defended. The door was reached by a removable gangway to a detached forestair rising about eight metres from the ground.

## The Basement

This small, dark, dungeon-like room may have been used sometimes as a prison, but it was mainly used as a storage-cellar. This would be of particular use when the Castle was under siege. For protection against enemies, the only entrance to the cellar was through a hatchway from the floor ubove. Ventilation came from a narrow openings in the walls. The south window has fairly recently been enlarged to become the present entrance to the Castle, while a stone stairway up to the kitchen has been added for the use of visitors. There was also a well in the centre of the floor, as water would be essential during a siege.

## The Kitchen

Above the cellar is the kitchen which has a "barrel-vaulted" roof to give more strength. It is a dark room, for the windows are also very small. The one in the south wall has a "slop-sink" with a runnel to carry dirty water to the outside; the other two have window seats. The fireplace has a salt-box at the back where salt would be kept dry. In the corner of the opposite wall there is a "garderobe", or primitive toilet, with a seat and a flue to the outside. In the north wall there is double recess which would probably be a cupboard.

## The Main Hall

This huge room is above the kitchen and, as has already been mentioned, was entered by the outside stairway. There were originally two doors, the inner one being fitted with a cross-bar. Inside the doorway there was a narrow space called The Screens, between a partition wall and the outer wall. This would provide more privacy for the family and, no doubt, protection from cold draughts. The size of this narrow area may be judged from the position of the two corbels, or support stones, high up in the side walls; these supported the beams for the partition. In the floor of The Screens there was a large trap-door ( the opening of which can still be seen ) through which stores were lowered to the kitchen, and from there to the cellar.  At the southern end of The Screens there is the circular stair leading down to the kitchen and up to the floors above.

The main hall has a large fireplace in the west wall, with a window beside it.  The other windows, also deep-set and provided with window-seats, give fine views of the Loch and the surrounding hill.  ( Some of Mary's biographers describe her prison and the Loch as dreary, cold and forbidding, but local people know that the moods of the Loch are constantly changing, and it can also be beautiful in tranquil sunshine )

**The Solar**

The floor above the main hall, which is called the Solar, is reached by the circular stair.  It has a fireplace and four windows and the east window has been used as an oratory for private prayer.  The Solar appears to have been divided into a sitting room on the east side, and one or two bedrooms on the west side.

**The Castle as a State Prison**

After the unsuccessful siege by Sir John Stryvelyne, the Castle was used as a State prison for important political offenders like John of Lorne, who was Lord Admiral and was sent there after the Battle of Bannockburn in 1314; he died in the Castle.  In 1368 the Steward of Scotland, who later became King Robert 11, and his son, the notorious "Wolf of Badenoch", were prisoners there. In 1431 Archibald, Earl of Douglas, was imprisoned for a short time by James 1.  Some years later "the unfortunate and virtuous" Patrick Graham, the first Archbishop of St Andrews, was imprisoned and died in the Castle.  He was later buried on St Serf's Island.

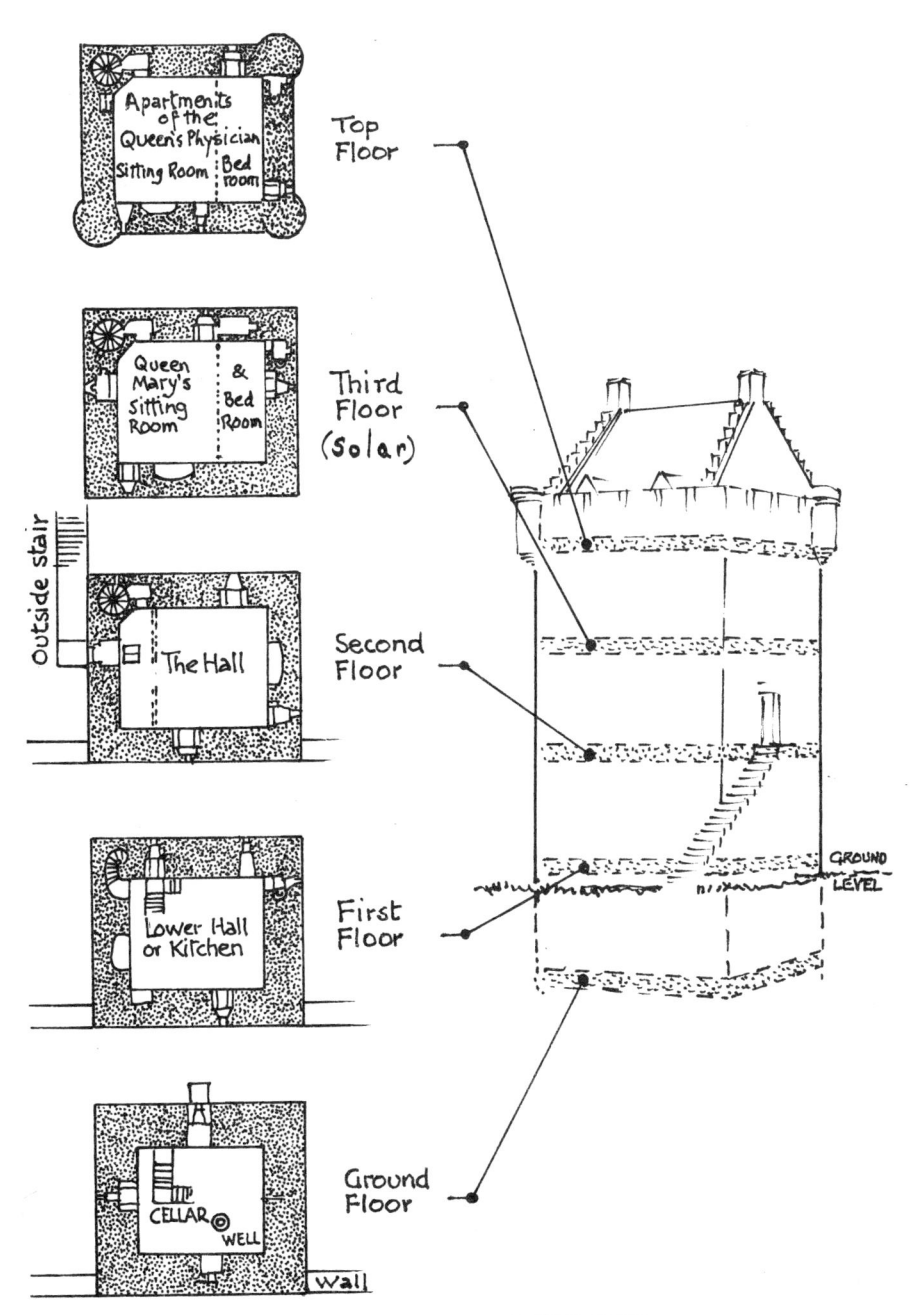

*ELEVATION OF THE TOWER KEEP*
By ANDREW THORBURN D.A.

## CHAPTER 2

## THE CASTLE AS QUEEN MARY KNEW IT

**Within the Walls**

Against the north wall there is a row of ruined buildings. The part nearest the postern gate was probably a guard-house, while the other part consisted of two rooms. The inner room contains a fire-place and an "aumrie", or cupboard, that might have been used for food or arms. The outer room has a garderobe.(The steps leading to the parapet walls were modern, but are no longer used)

**The "Presence Chamber"**

On the west side of the courtyard are the foundations of three buildings dating from the 16th century; the most interesting of these has obviously been a large hall with a fire-place and several windows, including a large one looking west towards Kinross. When this hall was described by Mr Burns-Begg in 1887, well-cut mouldings could be seen round the fire-place and windows.

The hall appears to have been over ten metres long, five and a half metres broad and nearly five metres high. He suggests that this could have been purpose-built as a Presence Chamber for the use of Queen Mary when she visited the Castle more than once between 1561 and 1565. Loch Leven was one of her favourite resorts for hunting with falcons.

The other small buildings attached to this so-called Presence Chamber appear, according to Mr Burns-Begg, to have been a kitchen with an oven beside it. In those days, when people of high degree travelled round the country, they took with them their own cooks and other servants, as they were afraid of being poisoned just as important people nowadays have body-guards to protect them from being assassinated.

**"The Glassin Tower"**

In the south-east angle of the ramparts there is a small, round tower with an entrance from the courtyard. Like the large hall, it was built in the 16th century, possibly by Sir Robert Douglas,

GROUND PLAN of the CASTLE
(adapted from plan made in 1901 by John Begg)

1. The Keep
2. "Glassin Tower"
3. "Presence Chamber"
4. Kitchen ?
5. Oven ?
6. Bakery ?
7. Oven ?
8. Landing Stages ?

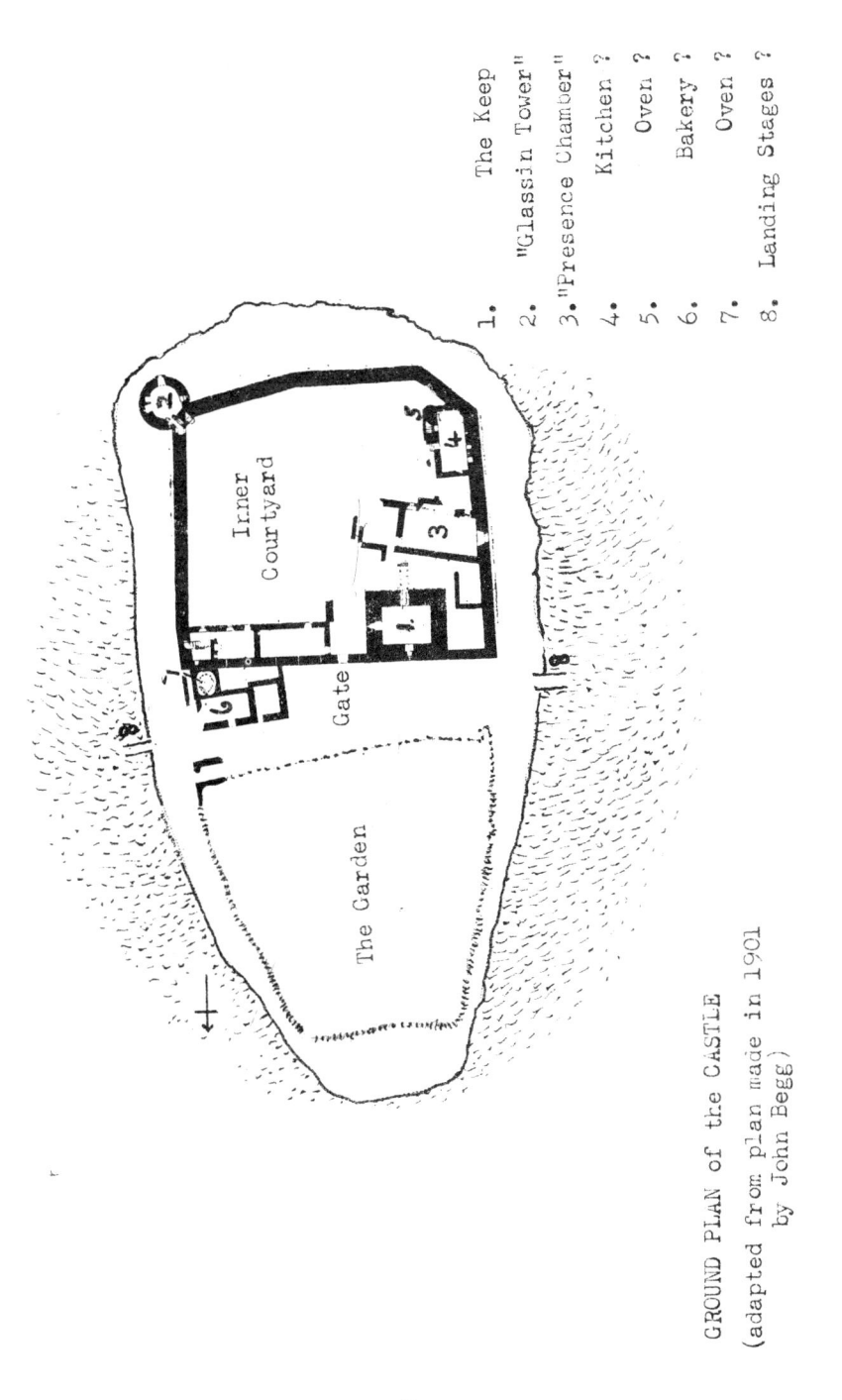

when he married Lady Margaret Erskine; a lintel stone bearing the carved initials "R.D. M.E." was found in the courtyard.

For some reason this tower was traditionally referred to by local people as "The Glassin Tower", or "The Glass Tower". Perhaps it was the only building in the locality to have glass windows at that time. The ground floor has a vaulted ceiling and there is a water inlet and slop-sink, so it may have been the servants' quarters. The room above is more ornate and has a fine oriel window facing south. Above this room is an apartment which seems to have been a bed-chamber, as there are two shallow alcoves or recesses for beds, and a garderobe. The only access to these two rooms was by a doorway leading directly from the courtyard into a small lobby, on the right-hand side of which there is a short flight of stone steps leading to the apartment above. The top chamber can be entered only from the parapet walk, so it was probably for the use of the watchmen only.

Mr Burns-Begg suggests that this tower may also have been built to the Queen's command, to give her more privacy during her short holidays on the Island.

**For Her Majesty's Comfort**

Mr Burns-Begg tells us that the Queen's apartments were, according to contemporary documents, quite magnificent as well as comfortable. The walls were hung with beautiful tapestries depicting scenes of hunting and hawking; her bed of green velvet was fringed with silk and had a taffeta counterpane. There was in her Presence Chamber a throne which had a canopy covered with crimson satin and figured with gold. The curtains were also fringed with gold and silver silk.

In her chamber Mary had a small ebony sofa and several chairs These, according to Mr Burns-Begg writing in 1887, were still to be seen in Dalmahoy, the home of the Earl of Morton who was descended from Sir William Douglas of Lochleven.

According to "The Inventory of Moveables of the Earl of Murray", compiled in 1561 (when Mary was newly returned from France) the preparations included:

"Four dossin of pewtar plaittis daliverit to George Hog, to take to Loich Levyn at the Queenis coming there" and also:

"Four dossin quhyt irne plaittis and four courtings of yellow atfiteis (taffeta) with ane frontell (pelmet ?) of the samyn."

## Relics of the Queen's Regalia

Miss Agnes Strickland in her book, "The Queens of Scotland", tells us that:

"Relics of Queen Mary were discovered when the Loch was partially drained in 1831. One of these was a sceptre with a carved stem, hilted with ivory and mounted with silver. It had probably formed part of her travelling regalia in happier days when she visited Lochleven, where she had a throne and cloth of estate, and occasionally held receptions...."

"A gold or richly-gilt key, with a Gothic bow, highly decorated, damasked all over with engraved flowers, having the date 1565 deeply cut along the outward ridge of the wards.... was found at the same time.... It is about four inches long with a pipe too wide for any ordinary lock; and from its ornamental character and the inscription must have been her Lord Chamberlain's badge of office and was probably lost by Sir Robert Melville in one of his voyages to or from the Castle."

## The Queen's Early Visits

The first of the visits of Mary Queen of Scots to Lochleven Castle of which there is any special record was in the spring of 1563. She rode from Falkland Palace to Kinross on the 9th of April and remained there until the 15th. She rode out hawking on the mainland and, on one occasion, when hunting near Turfhills, she paused to have conversation with John Knox, the Calvinist leader.

Mary's next visit to the County was in July 1565, when she was travelling from Perth to Edinburgh with her newly-wed husband, Lord Darnley, and his father, the Earl of Lennox. A plot had been hatched by some Scottish Lords to kidnap the Queen and take her to Lochleven Castle. The ambush was to be set at Paranwell on the west side of Benarty Hill, about two miles south of Kinross. But her loyal subject, Squire Lindsay of nearby Dowhill Castle, learned of the plot and rode post-haste to Perth to warn the Queen.

To avoid capture, the party set off early from Perth and had passed by Paranwell before the ambush was prepared.

(In 1838 at the suggestion of his friend, Sir Walter Scott, the Hon. William Adam of Blairadam House erected a commemorative archway or folly-bridge over what may have been the original highway, and near the spot where the ambush was to have taken place)

Two months later, on the 9th of September, the Queen and Darnley arrived at Kinross accompanied by an armed force. They ordered Lady Margaret Douglas and her son, Sir William, to surrender the Castle. But as Sir William was reported to be ill, and his daughter-in-law about to have a baby, the Queen allowed them to remain. Would she have been so lenient if she had had foreknowledge of what was to happen two years later?

During the following autumn, Lord Darnley spent a hunting holiday with his friend, Lord Burleigh at Burleigh Castle. His host must have complained about poachers spoiling the sport, as Darnley wrote a stiff letter to Sir William commanding him to take steps to prevent poaching on or around the Loch.

The last time Mary Stuart came to Lochleven Castle was on the 17th of June 1567. This time she was a lonely prisoner in the hands of two rough and merciless men who cared not whether she lived or died.

# CHAPTER 3

## EVENTS LEADING TO MARY'S IMPRISONMENT

### The Child Queen

Mary was born in Linlithgow Palace in 1542. She was the only surviving legitimate child of King James V; he was a nephew of the powerful King Henry Vlll of England, who was determined to take over Scotland as part of his own kingdom. Mary's mother, also called Mary, was a daughter of the Duke of Guise, a French nobleman. As France was almost at war with England at that time it was unlikely that the new baby's life would be a peaceful one.

That same year, after James had failed to obey Henry's command to attend a conference at York, the English army invaded Scotland and defeated the Scots at Solway Moss; many Scottish nobles were either killed or taken to England as prisoners. Broken-hearted, James went into retreat at Falkland Palace, and while he was there he heard of the birth of his daughter. He is said to have declared "It cam' wi' a lass, it will gang wi' a lass." Six days later he turned his face to the wall and died, leaving this new-born girl as his heir. She was crowned Queen when only nine months old.

### A Divided Nation

There was now the vital question of who was to rule Scotland as Regent while Mary was too young to do so herself. Her mother wanted Cardinal David Beaton, the Archbishop of St. Andrews. He and the Catholic nobles looked to France for help against the English.

On the other side was a Protestant, pro-English group of nobles, led by James Hamilton, the 2nd Earl of Arran, who was supported by leaders of the Scots Kirk. He eventually became the Regent, but, being a very weak character, did not keep a firm hand on the helm of State.

Among the Protestant Lords was James Stewart, the eldest of James V's illegitimate sons, and a half-brother to Queen Mary. His mother was Lady Margaret Erskine who married Sir Robert Douglas of Lochleven Castle.

## The Rough Wooing

When Mary was still less than a year old, Henry Vlll decided that she should marry his five-year-old son, Edward. At first Mary's mother was agreeable because Henry promised to allow Scotland to remain independent, and it was agreed that the marriage would take place when Mary was ten years old. But the Earl of Arran, who had been made Regent, changed sides and joined the Catholics. Henry then insisted that the child-Queen must go immediately to England. When this was refused, Henry's soldiers invaded and defeated the Scots at the Battle of Pinkie Cleuch in 1547.

In 1548 Cardinal Beaton was murdered by Protestant extremists (not without reason, for he was a very worldly prelate) so, although Henry Vlll had died a year earlier, it was decided that Mary would be safer in France.

As a result of Henry's "rough wooing", Mary had been hidden away on the Island of Inchmahome in the Lake of Menteith for three weeks, then moved secretly to Stirling Castle and from there to Dumbarton. Her mother would have been very happy to return to France, but she remained in Scotland to control matters for her daughter's sake.

## The French Connection

In 1548 Mary left Scotland, attended by her four Maries : Mary Fleming, Mary Seton, Mary Beaton and Mary Livingston. They arrived safely at the French Court, where they lived until 1561. Mary was proclaimed "the most beautiful princess in Europe", and soon settled happily into the cosseted, luxurious life of the French Royal Family.

Mary was married in 1557, at the age of fifteen, to the Dauphin Francis, who was a year younger. He was the eldest child of King Henri 11 and his Queen Catherine de Medici, so he was heir to the throne of France. Life was pleasant and carefree until 1559, which was a sad year when, first of all, Mary heard of the death of her beloved mother in Scotland, then King Henri died. Francis and Mary were now King and Queen of France; but the delicate young King also died a year later and Mary became merely the Dowager Queen, much under the power of Catherine de Medici.

### Claimant to the Throne of England

Meanwhile, in 1558 Mary Tudor of England, who was a Catholic, died and was succeeded by her half-sister Elizabeth 1, who was a Protestant. The Catholics in England, France and Spain argued that if Mary Tudor was Henry Vlll's true daughter, her mother being Catherine of Aragon, Elizabeth 1 must then be the illegitimate daughter of Henry and Anne Boleyn, who was beheaded. Therefore the rightful Queen of England must be Mary Queen of Scots, grand-niece of Henry Vlll (there were no male heirs)

For some time Mary displayed on her coat of arms and her silverware the rose of England together with the thistle of Scotland and the fleur de lis of France. In August 1561 Elizabeth was asked to acknowledge Mary as her heir-apparent.

Elizabeth was furious, especially when Mary usurped her coat of arms. She said she did not hate Mary, as others were to blame, but as long as Elizabeth lived there would be no other Queen of England. She went on to declare that the Scottish nobles' demand for her to acknowledge Mary as her successor was like asking her "to cover my eyes with my own winding sheet. No other Prince was ever asked to do such a thing."

From this time onwards Elizabeth was secretly Mary's bitter enemy. Not only was she angry at the claim to the English crown, but she was also at great risk from Mary's French and Scottish supporters, and even from her own Catholic subjects. She envied Mary for being younger (by nine years) and more beautiful, and for having borne a son and heir, while Elizabeth remained "but barren stock".

Nevertheless, because royal state politics of those days were full of intrigue and deceit, Elizabeth did not openly admit her true feelings, and in her letters she addressed Mary as "My dearest sister" or "My sweet cousin" (In actual fact, Elizabeth was cousin to Mary's father) Yet, when returning to Scotland, Mary was refused a safe-conduct pass through England, and on their voyage from France her ships had to run the gauntlet of the English fleet.

**The Four Maries**

The Queen arrived at Leith in the middle of August 1561. On board her own galley were her four young companions who had been with her since Inchmahome and during the seventeen years in France (Each Mary received 200 French livres per annum as payment for her service) Over these years they had blossomed into delightful ladies. Mary Beaton was considered the most beautiful, but Mary Fleming had greater charm and vivacity; Mary Livingston was full of energy and loved dancing, while Mary Seton was quiet and devoutly religious.

>"Yestreen the Queen had four Maries,
>Tonight there'll be but three.
>There's Mary Seton and Mary Beaton
>And Mary Carmichael and me."

Miss Strickland had a theory that "me" referred to a Mary Hamilton who was not one of the Queen's companions; she was a serving-maid who was seduced by one of the Court doctors, bore him a child and was "hanged in the High Street of Edinburgh" for adultery. The writer of the ballad about this poor girl has his facts wrong. Nor does history record a Mary Carmichael, but perhaps the name fitted better than Livingston.

## Return to Scotland

Two misfortunes turned what should have been a happy occasion into a dismal affair, which did not hold out much promise for the young Queen's future among her own people. First of all there was, unusually for August, a very thick and long-lasting "haar" or Scotch mist like a wet blanket over the Firth of Forth. Secondly, in their haste to escape capture by the English, Mary's ships arrived early, so the people of Leith and Edinburgh were not ready to welcome her. To give some extra time for the last minute preparations, the Queen and her retinue rested for a few hours in the home of Andrew Lambie, a wealthy Leith merchant, then they set off on a procession through the wet streets, accompanied by the Scottish nobles and their armed escorts.

Mary's favourite palfrey (on which she would have ridden side-saddle, a style new to Scotland) had been carefully embarked at Calais but had been captured by an English warship. Pierre Brantôme, the French chronicler, tells us that Mary wept to see the wretched horses provided for the procession. But there can be no doubt that the Queen would have tried to smile warmly as she waved to the bedraggled citizens cheering her on the two-mile journey to Edinburgh.

On the other hand, she certainly would not have smiled when her progress was stopped by a deputation of Craftsmen and their apprentices, craving her royal pardon for the ring-leaders in a recent riot during which "the gibbet had been dinged doon, and the Provost and Baillies locked up in Alexander Guthrie's writing-booth", the Tolbooth burst open and all the prisoners set free. The apprentices had been rescuing their friend, James Kellone, who had been sentenced to death for dressing up as Robin Hood on a Sunday.

Mary was so horrified at the severity of the punishment that she immediately pardoned Kellone. This generous gesture delighted the crowd, but angered some of the Protestant Lords and the Kirk leaders. John Knox later wrote, somewhat grudgingly, in his diary: "The Queen was that evening in her hall of Holyrood the most popular of sovereigns, for the moment.... while outside, in spite of the fog, there were bonfires of joy and cheering."

Brantôme, being a genteel Frenchman, turned up his nose at the uncouth Scots and wrote, "The evening serenade was the very completion of the day's disagreeables.... there came under her windows of Holyrood five hundred or six hundred rascals of the town to serenade her with vile fiddles and rebecks.... and singing so ill and in such bad accord that there could be nothing worse." In fact, Mary had to move to apartments away from the ground floor to escape from the noise.

After being installed in the Palace, Mary began to practise openly the rites of the Catholic Church in her worship. Opposition therefore grew stronger and more outspoken among the Protestants, and none was more outspoken than John Knox.

### To Be a Man with a Jack and Knapskull

For the next few years Mary settled into her new role as Queen of her small and turbulent country. She travelled with a large retinue of courtiers and servants from one castle to another and, if she found the accommodation poor in comparison with that offered in France, she was too diplomatic and too exhilarated to complain.

In 1562 the over-weight Lord Huntly in north-east Scotland was becoming too big for his boots, both mentally and physically. He was the acknowledged leader of the Catholic Lords and was beginning to take liberties frowned upon by the Protestants. It was therefore decided that Mary, accompanied by her half-brother Moray, should make a royal tour of the accessible northern areas and, if possible, remind Huntly that he was subject to the Queen's authority. Mary entered into this adventure with real enthusiasm. Huntly's Castle at Inverness was besieged and captured and the governor was hanged; Huntly himself fell dead of a heart attack during a skirmish near Aberdeen.

While taking part in this and another campaign later in the

north, Mary thoroughly enjoyed the outdoor life and bracing air of the Highlands. She wished she were a man to be able to lie out under the stars at night and to march along the highway wearing "a jack and knapskull" (a leather jacket and steel helmet) a shield and broad-sword.

## "Jezebel" and "The Calvinist"

On one of her sporting visits to Lochleven Castle, in 1563, Mary gave an audience to John Knox, who raged at her for not enforcing the very strict laws which had been passed by the Kirk Assembly against the Scottish Catholics. This was but one of many long, heated and unprofitable discussions between the Queen and the preacher, for there was then as much bigotry and mutual hatred between Catholics and Protestants in Scotland as there is now in Northern Ireland.

During a difficult two hours, the Queen remained in control of the discussion, and does not appear to have shown much resentment towards the outspoken reformer. The following day she summoned Knox to meet with her at Turfhills while she was hawking on horseback. On this occasion she presented Knox with a small watch within a crystal case, as a mark of her thanks for his help in settling a domestic quarrel between her friends, the Earl and Countess of Argyll, who were members of Knox's congregation.

In 1559 Knox had published a book entitled "First Blaste of the Trumpet Against the Monstrous Regimen (Rule) of Women". Nowadays he would have been denounced as a "male chauvinist pig", and as a hypocrite, because he was very careful to point out to the powerful Queen on the English throne that he had not been referring to her. Yet in his favour it must be said that, whatever his own shortcomings, he demanded a high standard of moral behaviour from his followers, and it was he who laid the foundations of our fine system of local schools and higher education which made Scotland the envy of the world for many generations.

To Knox, the young Queen was "immoral" because she insisted on celebrating the Catholic Mass, and because at her court there were the evils of feasting, dancing, card-playing and displays of jewelled finery, while the common people lived in abject poverty. In Mary's favour it might be said that she did not attempt to force the Catholic rites upon the nation, and the importation of a higher standard of living from France was of benefit to Scotland in the long run.

So, as is often the case, there was right as well as wrong on both sides, and if greater tolerance and consideration had been shown by one side for the other, the history of Scotland might have been happier.

*JOHN KNOX*
(anon.)

## CHAPTER 4

## MARY'S SECOND AND THIRD MARRIAGES

"Twelve daggeres were in him all att once"

In 1565 Mary married Henry Stuart, Lord Darnley. He was a tall, handsome, spoiled young man who was only nineteen years old. He was, however, of royal blood of both England and Scotland being, like Mary, a grandchild of Margaret Tudor, the sister of Henry Vlll. Darnley, who was the son of the Earl of Lennox, had spent many years in England, so had little in common with the Scottish nobles. For their part, they resented the title "King Henry" given to him by his wife after they were married.

The Earl of Moray rebelled against his half-sister and Darnley; he was defeated in "The Roundabout Raid" and outlawed. He fled to England, where he received cold comfort from Elizabeth, who did not approve of rebels or of failures.

In 1566 Mary was eagerly awaiting the birth of her first child, the heir to the throne. But love between the Queen and her husband had grown cold, and it was whispered to Darnley by her enemies (very probably without truth) that she was the mistress of her trusted Italian secretary, David Rizzio, or Riccio. One evening, while Mary was having supper with a party of friends in her apartment in Holyrood, they were interrupted by Darnley and a group of armed men, among whom were the Earl of Morton and Lords Ruthven and Lindsay. They attacked Rizzio as he clung for protection to Mary's skirts, then they dragged him from the room and stabbed him repeatedly on the stairway outside.

Mary's so-called friends who were with her in the Palace, fled after the murder had been committed, especially when they heard the Earl of Moray was back from England and on his way to Edinburgh. The Provost of the City arrived at the gates of the Palace, wanting to know what was going on, and demanding to be admitted to the Queen's presence. But "The King" came out and told him that Rizzio had been plotting with the Catholics in

France and Spain. He also told the crowd who had gathered to show their loyalty by going home, and they obeyed his orders.

**"No more tears now. I will think upon revenge"**
Now Mary was alone, a captive throughout the night in her own palace, with only one old lady to help her. Yet she controlled her anger and fear, and thought only about how she could manage to escape and take vengeance on her enemies. She knew that the murder had been set up to harm her and her unborn child, but for the baby's sake she forced herself to remain on friendly terms with her husband.

Together Mary and Darnley escaped from Holyrood and went to Dunbar, the home of the Earl of Bothwell, who was to play a very important part in Mary's life later on. A large troop of loyal supporters gathered at Dunbar, then Mary was escorted back to Edinburgh.

Soon the Queen had formed a Privy Council, consisting of Lords Moray, Argyll, Glencairn, Huntly, Athol and Bothwell.... an untrustworthy collection among whom were traitors and mutual enemies

**An Heir to the Throne**
In Edinburgh Castle in June of that year, Mary gave birth to a boy who, six months later in Stirling Castle, was baptised James. He was to become James Vl ("Jamie the Saxt") of Scotland; and because Elizabeth of England had no children, he might succeed to the throne of both countries. The Earl and Countess of Mar were appointed his governors, or foster-parents.

For some months after the birth, Mary was very ill, and near to death. After she had made it clear that, if she died, the next King would be her baby son and not her husband, Darnley left Stirling in a very bad temper and went to Glasgow to join his Lennox relations. Soon he was said to be plotting to capture the baby prince and seize the throne. Nevertheless, after Darnley fell ill in 1567, Mary installed him in a house at Kirk o' Field in Edinburgh, where they lived together quite peacefully for a short period.

One night, after Mary had left to go to Holyrood to attend a ball celebrating the wedding of her valet, Bastian de Pagès, Kirk o' Field was blown up by gunpowder. When Darnley's nearly-naked body was found in the garden, it had not been mutilated by the explosion, probably because Darnley had heard strange noises and had feared that the house was about to be set on fire, so he and his servant had already escaped. On the other hand, it is possible that he himself had had the gunpowder stored in the cellar, intending to blow up the house and kill the Queen; so, when he heard the noise of intruders he would know the imminent danger, and he and his servant would flee without waiting to dress.

There is little doubt, however, that Bothwell blew up the house; but who had strangled or suffocated Darnley in the garden ?

Once more Mary's health broke down under the shock of this murder, and despair at not knowing who had really killed Darnley. Eventually Bothwell was brought to trial, but he was found not guilty, partly because he brought a large troop of his own soldiers with him to Edinburgh, and partly because he had become the Queen's favourite. Meanwhile, the Earl of Moray had slipped away to France to avoid being mixed up in this affair.

*JAMES HEPBURN, EARL OF BOTHWELL*
(PHOTO ANNAN)
(By permission of the Scottish National Portrait Gallery)

**"Strange love they have given you"**

In April of that year Mary visited Stirling Castle and played for a short time with her baby son. They were never to see each other again.

>"My son ! My son ! may kinder stars
>Upon thy fortune shine !
>And may these pleasures gild thy reign
>That ne'er wad blink on mine ! "
>
>*(Robert Burns)*

On her way back to Edinburgh Mary was abducted by Bothwell, who took her to his castle at Dunbar. There they lived together for some time. Bothwell then divorced his wife, and eventually Mary agreed to marry him. Some historians say that she had fallen in love with him, others that she had no alternative as they were already as good as married.

We must remember that Mary's first husband, Francis, had been a delicate young boy, and a playmate for his young wife. Darnley was handsome and had polished manners, but he was conceited, petty and a drunkard. Now, perhaps she was swept off her feet by the vitality and strong personality of the robber-baron Bothwell, who carried her off to his castle and wooed her with the enthusiasm of a man who was determined to become King of Scotland.

This marriage brought no lasting happiness, but Mary remained loyal to her third husband. The common people greeted the marriage with amazement, anger and suspicion. A confederation of Lords, led by Morton, Argyll and Athol, raised an army to protect Mary and her son from the power-hungry Bothwell. They also sent an invitation to Moray to return to Scotland.

In June 1567, at Carberry Hill not far from Edinburgh, Bothwell and Mary found their army outnumbered. Bothwell fled to Dunbar, leaving Mary at the mercy of the Confederate Lords. She refused to denounce Bothwell, as she knew she was pregnant with his child. So Mary was carried back to Edinburgh, where the mob jeered and shouted insults, accusing her of murdering her second husband,

Darnley. Mary was held that night in lonely, humiliating captivity. At one point she opened the window and leant out calling for help, but she was dragged back inside and the window was firmly shut.

## Why Mary was Taken to Lochleven Castle

Mary had always shown great spirit and courage, and even at this desperate moment in her life, without a single friend to share her wretchedness, she reminded her captors that she was the Queen, and demanded an enquiry into the murder of Darnley.

The Confederate Lords had accused her of aiding Bothwell by luring Darnley to Kirk o' Field where he was killed. Bothwell had by now escaped to Scandinavia (where his life eventually ended in appalling conditions in a Danish dungeon) but his colleagues, including the Earl of Morton, were afraid that other facts might come to light if an enquiry were held, and they would be blamed too, so they decided to remove Mary from the public eye.

The people of Edinburgh, who had at first jeered the Queen, now pitied her, being shocked at the treatment she had received; for this reason also, it was decided to remove her from Edinburgh.

Moreover, her captors thought that, by holding her prisoner in Lochleven Castle, they might blackmail her into divorcing Bothwell in return for her freedom. They might also force her to abdicate the throne in favour of her baby son, so that Scotland could become a Regency, governed by her half-brother, James Stewart, the Earl of Moray, who might be better able to control the quarrelsome nobles and give to Scotland a period of stability.

The warrant for the Queen's imprisonment was signed by the Earls of Morton, Athol, Mar and others, and it committed her at first into the hands of two thoroughly nasty characters, Lord Lindsay of the Byres and Lord William Ruthven, whose father had taken part in the murder of Rizzio.

## Last Moments of Freedom

On the day following her humiliation at Dunbar, Mary had been taken back to Edinburgh and, to her joy, re-united with two of her Maries, Seton and Livingston. The Queen had eaten no food for three days, yet that evening her first meal was rudely interrupted by Morton, who ordered her to leave at once on horseback, taking nothing with her but a nightdress. Her two Maries were not allowed to go with her, only her chambermaids, Jane Kennedy and Maria Courcelles.

The party, led by Lindsay and Ruthven, travelled for at least four hours through the darkness as fast as the tired horses could be made to go. At first Mary thought she was being taken to Stirling Castle to be re-united with her child, James, but as dawn broke on the 17th of June 1567, she found herself on the shore of Loch Leven, where she was taken into custody by the Douglases.

# CHAPTER 5

## THE ROYAL PRISONER

**Mary's Jailers**

The Douglas family name had been associated with Lochleven Castle since Sir John Douglas had helped to defend it against Stryvelyne in 1335. In 1390 King Robert 111, the Steward of Scotland ( who had himself been a prisoner there for about a year) granted it by charter to Sir John's son, Henry Douglas, who had married the King's niece. He and his descendants were given the title of "Castellans of Lochleven". The building was really State property, and the family home was "The New House ( Manour ) of Loch Leven", which at that time stood on the mainland, to the north-east of the present Kinross House.

It has been suggested that, when this house was built, the villagers were forced to leave their primitive dwellings on the promontory, and move to new houses in the Sandport area. ( Similar steps were taken during the same period when Hamilton Palace and Scone Palace were being built ) This would ensure more privacy and wider policies for the Lord of the Manor.

Sir Robert married Lady Margaret Erskine, a niece of Henry V111, who became the mistress of King James V, Queen Mary's father, and bore him an illegitimate son called James Stewart, about 1531. This man was therefore the half-brother of Mary, who, in happier times, had granted him the title of Moray.

**The Laird**

In "The Scots Peerage" we read of Sir Robert: "On 20th January, 1540-41, he had a royal charter to himself in life-rent, and his son William in fee of the lands and barony of Kinross, with the castle and loch of Lochleven, the burgh of Kinross being erected into a burgh of barony."

Sir Robert and Lady Margaret had six children. After Sir Robert was killed at the Battle of Pinkie in 1547, their eldest son, Sir

William Douglas, became Castellan of the Castle, but usually received the title of "The Laird".

The Dowager Lady Margaret had always held that James Stewart, her royal son, should have been on the throne instead of his half-sister. So we can be sure that her welcome to the Queen was very cold. On the other hand, she would be determined that no harm should come to a captive in her care.

Sir William, being half-brother to the same James Stewart, and closely related to the Earls of Morton and Mar, could be trusted to guard the royal prisoner closely. His wife, Lady Agnes Leslie, was the daughter of the Earl of Rothes, who also supported James Stewart's claim to the throne.

The French novelist, Alexandre Dumas, in his historical novel, "Marie Stuart", tells us that Sir William was about thirty-five years old, a giant of a man with coarse features. His hair and beard were red, for he was a member of the "Red Douglas" family, who thought they had as much right to the crown as the Stewarts. Although his mother, Lady Margaret, had been the Stewart King's mistress, James V had always hated and feared the Douglases, and had driven them into exile in England. They did not return until after his death, and they never forgave Mary for her father's enmity.

The second son, George, was quite unlike the others, having blue eyes, black hair and a romantic nature. He and his elder brother disliked each other, and George was often absent.

One of Lady Margaret's daughters and a niece spied continuously upon Mary, even sleeping in her apartment. Another person determined to prevent the Queen's escape was a soldier named Drysdale, Captain of the Guard and an extreme Protestant, who developed a deep personal hatred of the Queen.

"Red Star of Boyhood's Fiery Thought"

At first the Queen was imprisoned in the Glassin Tower, which offered little comfort, as there had been no time to make preparations. Here Mary immediately suffered total collapse both mental and physical; for over two weeks she would hardly eat, drink or even speak, and it was feared that she might die.

But with characteristic courage she recovered and began to make the best of her captivity. She even managed to smuggle a few letters out to friends in Scotland and France.

In spite of these terrible experiences, and frequent bouts of ill-health, Mary was still enchanting. In 1569, for example, an English courtier described her in these words: "She.... hath withall an alluring grace, a pretty Scottische accente, and a searching wit, clouded with myldness." In appearance she was tall, slender and graceful, with a fresh complexion and auburn hair. She had long, delicate white hands. Her hazel eyes may have been a little too small, and her nose a little too big for her to have perfect beauty, but she had great vivacity, charm and dignity.

Mary was able to arouse the deep loyalty and sympathy of many of those around her on the Island, including even the Douglases. The second son, George, was one of these; he saw himself as her "Knight errant" and was determined to help her to escape.

Another young man who was to play an important part in this project was "The Foundling", Willie Douglas, who was sixteen years old. He was said to have been found abandoned as a baby in a boat beside the Castle. He may have been an illegitimate son of Sir William, with whom he was a favourite, and from whom he received a good education.

Even the old Dowager seems to have treated Mary reasonably and with consideration, and there were never any complaints from Mary of cruelty on her part. The Queen was given the freedom of the small garden, and she had her own private rooms in the Glassin Tower and her two ladies to wait upon her. Because of the constant fear of poison, Mary had her own cook and physician.

## "By friends deceived, by foes betrayed"

A frequent visitor to the Castle was her Equerry, Sir Robert Melville. Mary trusted him, but he was really on the side of the Confederate Lords, who sent him to Lochleven Castle in July 1567 to persuade her to sign away her throne.

On his first visit, the Queen might have listened to him, but Lindsay, Ruthven and the Laird insisted on being present during this conversation. The Queen was also very weak and distressed, so Melville left without her signature. A week later he returned alone and spoke with the Queen, but again without success.

During his third visit, between the 16th and 18th of July, he again urged the Queen to sign the papers, on the grounds that, if she did so, she would probably be set free and that afterwards she could disown her signature, claiming that she had signed under duress.

This time Mary showed more interest in Melville's advice, but when he also urged her to divorce Bothwell, who was now abroad as a fugitive, Mary would no longer listen to him. She knew she was going to have a baby who was Bothwell's child and, if she divorced the father, the child would have no royal future. She even asked Melville to deliver a letter to Bothwell, but this was refused because Melville was afraid of the Earl of Moray's anger. Mary tore up the letter and threw it into the fire.

A day or two later, the Queen gave birth to still-born twins, after which she was extremely ill with loss of blood.

# CHAPTER 6

## THE ABDICATION

"Woe worth thee, False Scottlande"

On the 24th of July Melville returned and entered the bed-chamber where the Queen lay very weak and distressed. He urgently advised her to sign the papers; then, carefully drawing his sword, he produced from the scabbard a folded message from Sir Nickolas Throckmorton, Queen Elizabeth's ambassador to Scotland, who also urged her, on Elizabeth's advice, to sign the Abdication.

After Mary had read this letter, Melville told her that her loyal Scottish supporters also wanted her to sign. He produced a turquoise jewel from the Earl of Athol, a tiny gold ornament from Lord Lethington, and a secret password from the Laird of Tullibardine; these were symbols of their loyalty. But, in spite of all appeals, Mary would not sign.

Waiting outside the Queen's room were the Lords Lindsay and Ruthven. They finally lost patience and stormed into the room, ordering Mary's two ladies to leave at once. They then forced the Queen to listen to the Deeds being read out by the lawyers who were to witness her signatures. Then they demanded that she put pen to paper, and Lindsay threatened to cut her throat if she refused.

In weakness, terror and despair Mary Stuart finally signed the Deeds of Abdication of the Scottish Throne in favour of her one-year-old son, and the granting of the Regency during his childhood to her half-brother, James Stewart, the Earl of Moray.

(It was Lord Lindsay, that noble gangster, who swiftly carried the documents to Edinburgh and forced the Keeper of the Privy Seal, Thomas Smelan by name, to seal them with wax using Mary's own seal of approval. Smelan did this under protest, his fingers trembling with fear)

After the others had left, Sir Robert Melville tried to calm her hysterical tears. He even suggested that escape was not impossible as young George Douglas was eager to help her, and was in a good position in the castle to do so.

Mary begged Melville to go to Edinburgh to find and rescue a diamond ring which had been given to her by Elizabeth in 1563 with a pledge to help Mary if ever she found herself in danger and returned the ring. Again, Melville refused because of his fear of Lord Moray. Mary later sent a letter to Elizabeth reminding her of this promise, but needless to say, there was no response. (Mr Burns-Begg tells us that Melville eventually found the ring and took it to Hamilton Palace soon after Mary had escaped from Lochleven)

*JAMES STEWART, EARL OF MORAY*
(By permission of the National Portrait Gallery of Scotland)

In Stirling on the 29th of July, Mary's son was crowned King James VI of Scotland. Sir William Douglas callously celebrated the Coronation by lighting bonfires and firing cannon on the Island. When Mary enquired what was causing the disturbance, he replied that she ought to be as happy as everyone else at the crowning of her own son.

We can be sure that, that night in the privacy of her room, Mary wept bitter tears.

**The Queen and the Regent**

Mary's next visitor was Moray, who had recently returned from France to be installed as Regent. Mary had always been conscious of the fact that he was her father's son and she had been, in her impulsive way, fond of him in spite of his treachery. It was she who had given him the vast lands of Moray, and she had even forgiven him for his part in the murder of Rizzio. But when he arrived on the Island on the 22nd of October, he was treated as royalty and as of higher rank than his half-sister. When he and the Queen met, on two consecutive days probably in the "Presence Chamber" and with great formality, Moray's cold disdain was deliberately insulting. Mary demanded to be allowed to appear in a Court of Law to justify herself against the accusation of having murdered Darnley. For a moment she actually cowed Moray with stinging sarcasm, accusing him of treason, and warning him that one day he would regret his deeds, as the common people could not trust him.

But such talk was rash, for he was a very dangerous enemy. He threatened Mary with execution and went off, leaving her in a state of great terror. Yet, in his presence the Queen would be able to conceal this fear, as she had the ability to appear calm and dignified even when faced with armed men. She had had plenty of practice!

**Brother Against Brother**

Moray was furious, and his rage spilled over on his half-brother George, whom he banned from the island forever. Sir William also ordered George to leave and not return. This was a hard blow to "The Escape Committee" but, before he left, George outlined to the Queen the details of a rescue attempt, and told her that Willie Douglas would take his place on the island.

Willie, who was now in charge of the Laird's boats, was still a young lad. He had a tendency to gamble, and he openly showed gold coins given to him by the Queen, which aroused suspicion. On one occasion he dropped a letter he was smuggling to Mary, and this was noticed and reported by one of the Douglas girls. Nevertheless, Willie was loyal to the Queen and his help would be essential.

George remained in or near the village of Kinross, and kept in touch with Willie Douglas by means of smuggled messages. On one occasion he rode his horse far out into the shallow loch, trying to get near enough to signal to the Queen in the garden. Sir William was so angry that he ordered the guards to fire a cannon-ball at his brother; fortunately this went over his head. Mr Burns-Begg reports that a very old cannon-ball was found on the shore near the island called Roy's Folly, which was not visible at that time. It lay, he explains, on the probable line of fire of a shot aimed at George when he was in a position to signal to someone in the garden. There is an old ball now in Kinross Museum which might well be the very one that Sir William fired at his brother.

When Moray returned to Edinburgh he confiscated many of the Queen's personal jewels and sold others to Elizabeth, particularly the unusual black pearls which were Mary's favourites. Her beautiful clothes and furniture soon had pride of place in the homes of the Confederate Lords, and her ornaments would be shown off in the "aumries" of their best rooms.

Much of her silver-plate was melted down and made into coins. Mary had intended her finest jewels to be added to the Honours of Scotland (which are exhibited in Edinburgh Castle) The huge diamond in shape of an "H" set in a ruby was to be added to the ancient crown; this jewel, nicknamed "The Great Harry", had been given to Mary by her father-in-law, Henri 11 of France, when she married the Dauphin. It was stolen by the Earl of Moray and was later worn by his widow; Parliament had great difficulty in getting it out of her clutches.

## "A Victim of Sad Strife"

Once again Mary became very ill, and she was frequently bedridden during the following months, her body beginning to swell and her skin to turn yellow. Poison was suspected, but this was unlikely as the Laird himself not only carried the food into her room, but also tasted it first.

Lady Antonia Fraser tells us that one antidote to poison, a piece of "horn of unicorn" sent from France, was dipped into each cup of wine and plate of food before Mary had her meal. The Queen seems to have had great faith in this talisman for she bequeathed it to her son before she died.

# CHAPTER 7

## A WEARISOME TIME

### The Gloomy Tower

After the Abdication had been signed, Mary expected that the conditions of her imprisonment might be made less unpleasant but, on the contrary, she was now transferred to the Solar storey of the main tower, above the great Hall, while her personal doctor occupied the pent-house under the roof. Her rooms were larger, but there was much less privacy.

Lady Antonia Fraser tells us that in June Mary had requested better clothes for herself and her maids, and as a result she received a red satin petticoat edged with fur, some satin sleeves, a pair of silk stockings, some pins and some sweets. During the following months, more parcels arrived containing clothes, sweets and small ornaments, as well as soap and powder, handkerchiefs and a little French alarm clock.

Then at last there arrived her wigs, together with an embroidered cape for her to wear when they were being dressed by Mary Seton, who had learned the art while living at the French court; Seton had by now been allowed to rejoin her mistress.

Even in the days when her own auburn hair was naturally beautiful, the Queen wore "perruques" because they were fashionable in France. These elaborate confections of real hair must have been a source of wonder to the simple women-folk who guarded the Queen. They would wonder also at her dainty velvet caps trimmed with gold and jewels, and the jewelled crucifix she wore on a long gold chain round her neck. Her stockings were of silk and her shoes of finest leather or velvet.

### A Caged Bird

During the long months of autumn and winter there was a period of restfulness and quiet during which Mary's health recovered. She could no longer write letters, having neither paper nor ink, so she returned to her favourite pastime of embroidery. This work was done with coloured silks on taffeta, or with silver and gold thread on stronger materials such as velvet and linen. Her materials would probably be brought to her by Sir Robert Melville.

Mary sewed into the emblems and designs her burning anger at her persecution and martyrdom; she even embroidered gifts for Elizabeth and sent them like cryptic messages begging for help. In one of her designs, Mary shows herself as a caged bird with a menacing hawk above her, while in another she and Elizabeth are shown as two women astride the Wheel of Fortune. She sometimes sent to Edinburgh for threads, and for the services of an "Inbroiderer" to draw patterns and supervise the mounting of the completed tapestries. Mary became engrossed in her needlework and sewed until her fingers were aching.

Sir William Drummond of Hawthornden described in 1614 some of the Queen's handiwork. There is one device which shows a Phoenix rising from flames, with her own (and her mother's) motto in French: "En ma fin est mon commencement", which translates to "In my end is my beginning". Another motto, in Latin, signifies "Virtue flourishes as a result of a wound". There is one elaborate emblem consisting of a large "M" for Mary with the letters "R" and "S" (possibly for Regina Scotiae or Queen of Scotland) embroidered over it. Mary also delighted in making anagrams from the letters of her name, and one of these was "Tu as Martyre" which means "You have Martyrdom".

Most of these items would be embroidered while Mary was in prisons in England, but some may have been worked while she was languishing in Lochleven Castle. Mr Burns-Begg identified one specimen of her needlework as a folding screen "now at Dalmahoy House", which he believed might be the very work that Mary was doing just before she escaped.

"But I, the Queen of a' Scotland, maun lie in prison strang."
Brantôme tells us that Mary enjoyed singing, in her clear and pleasant voice, to the music of her lute. She enjoyed playing

chess, billiards and card-games. She was also fond of dancing so, during the long dark evenings, she may on occasion have joined her jailers in a French galliard or Scottish reel. To the Douglases and their servants the Queen would speak in the "Lallans" Scots dialect, but to Mary Seton and the doctor she would probably speak French. She had been bi-lingual even as a child, for her mother spoke French while her father used the Lallans (Gaelic was spoken mainly in the Highlands and the countryside)

In happier times the Queen had enjoyed croquet, archery and the national game of golf, and she was an accomplished horsewoman so the narrow confinement of her life on the Island must have been a form of torture.

Prayer was a great solace to the Queen, who spent some time every day in the little recessed oratory in the east wall of the Solar. She was fond of reading, being fluent in French, Italian and Latin, and was particularly fond of French poetry. The Queen herself composed some verses. A Sonnet written by Mary in 1568 to Elizabeth (possibly from Lochleven) contains these tragic words:

> "A longing haunts my spirit day and night,
> Bitter and sweet, torments my aching heart.
> Between doubt and fear, it holds its wayward part,
> And while it lingers, rest and peace take flight."

Sometimes Mary felt too unwell to enjoy any activities. She complained of severe headaches and other pains, and spells of fainting. Lady Antonia Fraser is of the opinion that the Queen suffered from porphyria (a rare disease, which may have been inherited by James her son) The symptoms were periodic outbursts of hysteria, and acute pains in the stomach and joints which her doctor attributed to colic and rheumatism.

On her "good" days however, Mary might walk in the tiny garden, gazing longingly towards the shore from whence help must come if she were to escape.

QUEEN MARY IN HER ROOM
By John Begg 1887

## The Torment of Delay

By May the "Escape Committee" had become active again. There were by now more people in the castle prepared to help the Queen. These included Mary Seton, Jane Kennedy and two of the younger Douglas girls who had become devoted to her; and it is obvious that some of the menials, particularly the women, had taken pity on the prisoner, and would at least keep quiet if they suspected any attempt at escape.

The two young men, George and Willie Douglas, had already discussed the possibility of carrying the Queen off the island in a large box supposed to contain important papers; but it was soon clear that the Queen could not attempt this.

Another discarded idea was that of commandeering one of the coal-boats which carried fuel from the mainland to the island. One boat could easily carry about seventy men, who would attack the castle by night and carry off the Queen. Unfortunately, this proposed attempt came to nothing, because George told Drysdale, the Captain of the Guard, about this plan, not realising at that time that Drysdale would betray Mary and warn Sir William to have the coal-boats well guarded.

George next suggested that Mary might be able to jump down from a considerable height (either from the garden wall or from the oriel window in the Glassin Tower) The drop was nearly three metres, and when one of the Queen's ladies experimented by leaping, as if in fun, from a similar height within the courtyard, she damaged her ankle so badly that this idea had also to be abandoned.

The fourth suggestion was put into action: this was for Mary to leave the castle openly, disguised as the laundry-woman and carrying a bundle of laundry. Mary succeeded in changing into the woman's garments – a loose gown of "linsey woolsey" hanging straight from the shoulders, a rough plaid or shawl over her head, and simple hide shoes on her feet.

The plan went well at first and the Queen, carrying a "fardel" of laundry, reached the boat safely. Unfortunately, one of the boatmen was curious and tried to remove the shawl covering her face, where-upon Mary exposed her hands - those long, delicate white fingers which could never have belonged to a washerwoman - and the Queen had to return to "The Gloomy Tower". Fortunately the boatmen were persuaded to keep silent about this unsuccessful attempt.

Another setback came when the Laird, suspicious of Willie's activities, sent him packing off the Island; he also wrote to George warning him never to come near the Castle or even Kinross again.

In a footnote to Sir Walter Scott's novel, "The Abbot", we read that Mary stated in a letter to France that the guard, "Jasper Dryfesdale", had threatened to murder Willie and to plant a dagger in Mary's own heart.

**Would She Ever Regain Her Freedom ?**

We can easily imagine the Queen's despair at this time. To compensate for his harshness, Sir William tried to entertain the Queen, and even took her boating on the Loch. There was a suggested plot to rescue Mary if she could persuade her jailer to land a picnic party on St Serf's Island, but this was not given much serious thought.

The topic of the Queen's possible escape was openly discussed at this time, and Mary even treated it as a joke when speaking to the Douglas family; this, of course, was to make them believe that she would no longer consider escaping. Once when the Queen and Sir William were returning from an expedition on the Loch, they found the servants having fun by pretending to attack the Castle and free the Queen. But Drysdale went too far and discharged a loaded pistol, seriously wounding two of the soldiers.

The Queen arranged to have their wounds treated by her own doctor, who played his part in the escape plans by keeping the men in bed as long as possible.

George Douglas now informed his parents that he intended to go to France to seek his fortune. He asked permission to visit the Castle to bid them all farewell, and to ask the Queen to recommend him to her friends there. Lady Douglas, who was fond of George, was very upset by this and asked Mary to write a note to George and to persuade him not to go to France. Mary's letter was coded, and she actually urged George to hasten the plans for her own escape (This was now very difficult without the presence on the Island of either George or Willie Douglas)

A letter from Mary to Catherine de Medici, begging for help in the form of troops, was also smuggled out of Lochleven, but there was no response from her mother-in-law.

CHAPTER 8

THE RESCUE

**The Long-awaited Signal**

It was by now very obvious that the only possible means of escape was by obtaining the key of the postern gate in the rampart wall of the Castle. This, the only gate, was locked every evening at seven. The key was then taken to the Laird, who kept it carefully beside him. As soon as the gate was locked the guards were off duty, so this was the one time when the Queen might be able to escape unseen.

One of George's sisters, who was on the Queen's side, persuaded Sir William to allow Willie to return to the Island, and "The Foundling" came back on the 30th of April. The following day some fifty men, led by Lord Seton (Mary Seton's father) and John Beaton were on their way from Edinburgh to Kinross. Letters, probably written on Mary's silk handkerchiefs, using chimney soot for ink, were smuggled out to them by maids passing between the Castle and the New House or Kinross village.

Smuggled into the Castle was a pear-shaped pearl earring belonging to the Queen. This had been given to George before he left the Island and Mary knew that it was the long-awaited signal that her loyal friends were ready and waiting for her to reach the mainland.

**Nau's Memorials**

The following forty-eight hours must have been nerve-wracking for the Queen and those others who were involved.

We are lucky to have a very detailed, moment-by-moment account of what actually happened. This was written by a Frenchman, Claude Nau, who was the Queen's secretary from 1575 to 1586. In 1578 he began to write down, in French, what Mary told him about her escape. Although this was ten years after the event, we can be sure that she would remember every detail of what had been a traumatic experience, and there was no reason for the Queen to distort the facts.

Moreover, two other quite independent accounts of the escape were written. One of these, sent in 1568 by an Italian ambassador, Petrucci, to the Grand Duke Cosmo de Medici, and now in the Medici archives, is very similar in essential details to what Mary told to Claude Nau. The other is an anonymous account preserved in the Vatican, which also agrees with Nau's version.

Shortly after writing his "Memorials" Nau and another servant betrayed the Queen during an investigation into the Babington plot to murder Elizabeth. Although the men had probably been tortured, Nau had to leave for France immediately in disgrace. His "Memorials" lay undiscovered or unrecognised for nearly 300 years in the library of an English historian, Sir Robert Bruce Cotton of Ashburton House. This library was destroyed by fire in 1731, and the Cottonian Collection of coins and old manuscripts was removed to Westminster School and then to the British Museum.

The "Memorials" were found in 1883 and translated into English by a Jesuit priest, Father Joseph Stevenson. Mr Burns-Begg must have rejoiced to have access to this long-lost source of infcrmation about Mary Queen of Scots. Reading Nau's account is almost like listening to the Queen telling her own story.

**The Tension Mounts**

At first there were good omens: Sir William's wife had recently given birth to a child, so she would probably remain in her own room for some time; the two wounded soldiers were still under the care of the doctor; and Jasper Drysdale had been sent off to Edinburgh on an errand for the Queen, thinking that he was to collect for himself a sum of money from a friend of the Queen. But in this letter Mary asked her friend to delay Drysdale's return as long as possible.

Unfortunately, however, all these people returned to the castle sooner than had been expected.

On the 2nd of May young Willie, who was a great favourite with most of the Douglas household, pretended to celebrate his return by inviting everyone to a party (Mary had given him some money to pay for this) He craftily arranged that the feast would be held in that part of the courtyard from where they would not be able to see signals from the shore.

After the feast, Willie played a popular and traditional May Day game: he appointed himself "Lord of Misrule" or "The Abbot of Unreason", and announced that all to whom he gave a branch of leaves must do exactly as he ordered them. When he presented the Queen with her branch he ordered her to "Follow My Leader", while he behaved as if he were drunk or very silly. No doubt this could be used later as an excuse for any mysterious movements by Willie and the Queen.

At last the Queen, exhausted by these capers, lay down to rest. A short time later she overheard the woman who kept the Inn at Kinross gossiping with the Laird's wife, and telling her that a large body of mounted men had come to the village that day. They said they were on their way to an Assize or Law Court, but Mary knew that her friends had arrived. She was naturally anxious to see for herself any movements on the mainland, so she put on her cloak and went down to walk in the garden.


### A Cool Head
She was quickly joined by the Dowager Lady Douglas, who spoke for a short time. It was she who spotted the armed horsemen by the shore, and was about to raise the alarm when Mary, keeping very cool and pretending to be uninterested in the horsemen, began a lively argument with Lady Douglas about Lord Moray's unkind behaviour. This kept Lady Margaret engrossed in conversation until the men had disappeared. (It has been suggested that Lady Douglas had some hopes that her son George might marry the Queen after she escaped, and therefore may have deliberately turned a blind eye to the activities on the shore)

Mary delayed her supper as long as possible to allow Willie to complete his preparations. The food was brought to her room, as usual, by Sir William himself. While Mary was taking her meal he looked out of a window in the Solar and noticed Willie acting strangely among the boats. He was driving little pegs into the chains of every one except the Queen's escape boat, to prevent it from being followed.

Sir William yelled to Willie telling him to give up being such a fool. Again the Queen diverted attention by pretending to feel faint and begging for a glass of wine. The Laird being the only person present, he had to hurry off to fetch it himself, and this dangerous moment also passed.

At no time did Mary lose her nerve, and this was very important in the success of the escape.

After the Queen had finished her meal, the Laird went off to have his own supper with the family in the hall below. By a stroke of luck Drysdale, who usually guarded the Queen when the family were at supper, went out into the courtyard to play at handball. Now Mary had to get rid of the two young girls who had come to her room, as she was never left alone for long.

She made the excuse that she wished to pray privately and went upstairs to the doctor's room where, no doubt, she did pray for a short time, but very earnestly, for her delivery from captivity. Here she also changed quickly into a red gown belonging to one of the taller servants, and covered it with her own cloak. One of her maids was dressed in the same fashion, for she was to escape with the Queen, while the other lady remained with the girls in the Solar to keep them amused as long as possible during the Queen's absence.

"By a steel-clenched postern door"

As Sir William sat at table downstairs, the vital key lay beside his hand. While serving the meal, Willie dropped a napkin over the key and, un-noticed, picked up both together. He then signed to an accomplice to pass the word to the Queen, who swiftly slipped

- 46 -

down the circular stair and into the Screens, where she could not be seen from the main hall. Then she stole out through the Castle doors and down the outside stairway.

Here she and her companion waited, huddling close to the wall. Some of the servants may have noticed them but did not recognise the Queen, or if they did so, made no sign. When Willie joined them they walked more boldly to the postern gate, where he let them through and locked the gate from the outside, dropping the key into the mouth of a cannon which stood nearby.

The little group now waited here for a moment to be sure they had not been spotted from the windows, then they slipped into the boat where Mary lay down under the seat. Some serving-women were larking about near the pier, and one of them recognised Mary. She was about to cry out when Willie told her to hold her tongue, and fortunately she obeyed him.

*SKETCH OF THE CASTLE SHOWING THE POSTERN GATE*
(By permission of Kinross-shire Antiquarian Society)

**Local Legend**

Mr David Marshall was a Lochleven boatman and antiquarian, whose collection was gifted to form the original Museum of Kinross. When writing in his diary in January 1859, he stated that a weaver called William Honeyman pointed out to him the spot where he had found "the keys of Lochleven Castle" in 1805, when he was a boy of thirteen. Mr Marshall also reported that about 1830 or 31 a boy named James Drysdale, "perhaps a descendant of him who was in the Castle in Queen Mary's time" found a bunch of eight keys, five of which were of superior workmanship, on a châtelaine designed to be worn at a lady's waist. The hook was ornamented with a St Andrew's Cross. Mr Marshall believed that it had been worn by Jane Kennedy who, it was said, had swum from the island to join the Queen. Willie helped her into the boat, then Jane deliberately dropped her keys into the water. Willie soon followed suit, as if putting into action the words of Roland Graeme in "The Abbot":

"Now I resign my office of porter of Loch Leven, and give the keys to the Kelpie's keeping."

There is therefore a commonly-held belief that Willie threw the key into the Loch. Several large keys which were found are now exhibited in places like Kinross Museum, Provand's Lordship in Glasgow and Sir Walter Scott's home at Abbotsford. Each one may have been claimed as "the genuine article", but there is no historical evidence that Willie did throw the key into the water.

**Safe at Last**

Meanwhile, George Douglas and John Beaton, who had been at the local inn, supposedly on their way to Glasgow, made an excuse to go for a walk. As they came in sight of the Loch, they saw Willie's boat approaching the shore. Mr Burns-Begg thought it was probably heading for the landing-stage now called the Factor's Pier on the east side of Kinross House, but others have claimed that Mary landed where the water then lapped near the Sandport. The latter is more likely, as the pier beside the Sandport would be out of sight of the "New House of Kinross"

As he was rowing, Willie's passengers saw an armed man at the water's edge, and Willie stopped rowing in fear, until the man shouted that he was one of George's servants.

As soon as the Queen, her maid and Willie were on shore they were surrounded by friends, and the Queen was immediately mounted on a horse which George had stolen from the Laird's stables. Mary would not set out, however, until she had seen that Willie was also mounted; but her maid had to be left behind until a horse could be found for her.


**The Bird Has Flown!**
As she rode through the Sandport, Mary Queen of Scots was cheered by the common people, who had been enjoying a Sunday walk by the Loch. Mr Burns-Begg writes:
"One can easily imagine how readily and spontaneously expressions of kindly sympathy would be elicited from these groups as the mounted cavalcade rode past them, led by Queen Mary herself in all her striking grace and beauty, and flushed with the excitement of long-lost liberty regained."

The route would then be south on the old road by Cavelstone and Classlochie Farms, over the bridge at Coldon Farm and round by Paranwell on the original highway to the Queen's Ferry. Here the party was joined by Lord Seton and the Laird of Riccarton. From South Queensferry they rode south-west to the Castle of Niddry Seton, now called Niddry Castle, near Winchburgh in West Lothian.


**Meanwhile....**
Back at Lochleven Castle there was rage mingled with panic. Jasper Drysdale stormed like a madman, the Laird threatened to commit suicide, and Lady Douglas probably accused them both of being too lax in guarding Mary Stuart.

But Sir William seems to have survived this disgrace because, shortly afterwards, he was put in charge of the Castle's last prisoner, the Earl of Northumberland, one of Mary's supporters, whom Sir William surrendered to Elizabeth for £1000.

On the death of the 5th Earl of Morton in 1588, the Laird became the 6th (or was it the 7th ? ) Earl.  Lord Maxwell held the same title, and the two men came to blows over it in St Giles Cathedral in 1593; but Sir William prevailed in law.

In 1594 King James VI appointed him his lieutenant in the South of Scotland while His Majesty went North.  The Earl died in 1606, and his descendants continued to hold the Castle of Lochleven until 1675, when it passed to Sir William Bruce.  It was still habitable in 1650, but after that it gradually fell into ruins, "its towering strength grown ghostly".

## The Last Battle

From Niddry, Mary moved on immediately to Hamilton Palace, where large numbers of Lords, Bishops and common people rallied round her standard.  She was now able to declare publicly that her abdication had been invalid, because she had signed the deeds against her will.  She also wrote to the Regent Moray demanding that he resign his position.  But, of course, Moray would not consider this, and the stage was set for civil war between his and the Queen's supporters.

Less than a week later, Mary was to be found once more on horseback, on rising ground above the village of Langside near Glasgow, where a battle was being fought.  Although Mary's army was larger, her half-brother Moray's forces were better equipped and better led.  Moray's men, among whom Sir William Douglas distinguished himself, routed the Queen's forces, killing over 100 and taking prisoner many more.  And that was the end of Mary's hopes in Scotland.

> "Queen, for whose house my fathers fought
> With hopes that rose and fell."
>
> (Swinburne)

# CHAPTER 9

## TRAPPED IN ENGLAND

**Over the Border**

In desperation Mary fled south to Dundrennan Abbey on the Solway Firth near Kirkcudbright; and from there despite strong advice against it, she insisted in crossing over into England (Mary could never bring herself to believe that Elizabeth would not lift a finger to help her ) A small fishing-boat carried her across the Firth to the home of Sir Henry Curwen at Workington Hall. He was a Catholic so Mary was sure that she would be safe with him. But on Elizabeth's orders, Curwen handed her over to Carlisle Castle, the first of many prisons in which she was held during the seventeen years of her captivity in England.

Fourteen of these years were spent in Sheffield Castle and nearby Sheffield Lodge, and much shorter periods in Bolton, Tutbury, Chartley, Wingfield and, finally, Fotheringhay. Lady Antonia Fraser explains that these frequent transfers were partly due to the need for the servants to clean the buildings thoroughly. No doubt the open flues from the "garderobes" became very dirty, and the rooms would become infested with fleas, rats and other pests when overcrowded by Mary's large retinue. The frequent moves would also discourage attempts to free the prisoner.

**What Happened to "The Foundling" ?**

For the rest of his life Willie Douglas continued to serve his royal mistress in various ways. His duties included acting as her "usher" - walking ahead of the Queen and announcing her approach on formal occasions - and as her "chair-bearer", which probably involved carrying one end of the sedan chair which Mary used as illness increasingly prevented her from going on foot.

According to Mr Burns-Begg, Willie was "lost" in some prison or other for a short period while Mary was in Carlisle, but by 1570 he was helping to stir up a rebellion against Elizabeth in the North of England. He even went to France in 1571 and spoke on Mary's behalf to her brother-in-law, the Emperor Charles 1X, and the Queen-mother, Catherine de Medici.

Mr Burns-Begg wrote of Willie Douglas:
"His name as the youthful liberator of his unfortunate Queen will ever occupy a prominent place in Scottish History."

**George Douglas, the Knight-errant**

George also continued to serve the Queen. He was with her at Langside and accompanied her to England. She sent him to France to seek help, and while there he fell in love with a French lady. Mary wrote him several letters, encouraging his "affaire de coeur". But as she had no money, she was unable to give George the financial aid he needed to win the lady's hand.

He returned eventually to Scotland and settled down to a more peaceful life. According to "The Scots Peerage", he married twice. His first wife was Jonet ( not Janet ) Lindsay of Dowhill, whom he married about 1575. George's second wife was Margaret Durie, widow of William Scott of Abbotshall, who may well have been an ancestor of the famous historical writer whose novel "The Abbot" deals with Queen Mary's imprisonment in Lochleven Castle.

By 1602 George had become Sir George Douglas of Helenhill and Rumgally. He had a charter from his brother William of the lands of Ashieshiels near Peebles in 1589. Latterly he lived in "Dean's Court" in St Andrews.

### "My Dearest Seton"

When Mary Seton also rejoined the Queen at Carlisle, she would be much distressed to discover that the Queen had cut short her hair during the flight from Langside. Seton's first task would be to dress a wig fittingly for a still-royal personage, and her presence must have been a great comfort to Mary especially as Seton was the most cultivated and talented of her Maries. She was the daughter of the 6th Lord Seton, and her mother was a French lady who had been maid-of-honour to Queen Mary's mother.

Seton served Mary faithfully for 35 years. She was a devout Catholic and the only one of the four to remain unmarried. She retired in 1583 while Mary was in Sheffield Castle, and went to France where she entered a convent near Rheims. She lived on for nearly 30 years after the death of her mistress, so she must have been well over 70 when she died in lonely, poverty-stricken exile from the Scotland she loved.

### The Casket Letters

In June 1567, three months after Lord Darnley had been murdered in Kirk o' Field, Lord Morton declared that a silver casket had been discovered in the house of a tailor named George Dalgleish. Within this casket there were reported to be papers concerning Bothwell. Morton did no more about these letters at that time, nor did he mention that there were letters from the Queen among them, which incriminated her in the murder of her second husband.

In December of that year, while Mary was in Lochleven Castle, it was made public that the Casket Letters proved that the Queen had plotted with Bothwell, and had written to Darnley inviting him to Kirk o' Field so that Bothwell could murder him. Therefore Mary was also guilty of this murder. Yet these accusations could and should have been made six months earlier, and neither in June nor in December was Mary told of the discovery of the letters.

### The Conference of York

Then in October 1568, while Mary was in Bolton Castle, the Regent Moray took the Casket Letters to York, where Mary was to be tried on a charge of being implicated in Darnley's murder. The trial was a mockery, as Mary was allowed neither to attend nor to read the letters she was alleged to have written.

It was at this time also that George Buchanan, scholar and Protestant reformer, produced false and disgusting accounts with which the Regent hoped to prove Mary's guilt, and so obtain her return to Scotland.

At York, the Law Lords could find no firm proof of Mary's guilt Elizabeth then ordered the legal proceedings to be transferred to Westminster; but still there was no guilty verdict. Mary remained a prisoner in Bolton while her half-brother returned to Scotland. The Casket Letters mysteriously disappeared soon afterwards.

### All Hope is Lost

At first Mary's courage, optimism and faith kept her spirits strong and her hopes high that Queen Elizabeth would release her, or that her friends would help her to escape. But these hopes gradually died.

In 1570 news came from Scotland that the Regent Moray had been assassinated by a Hamilton ( who was liberally rewarded by Mary) Two years later, thousands of Protestant Huguenots were massacred in France on the eve of St Bartholomew's Day, on the orders of a group of nobles among whom was Mary's cousin, the Duke of Guise. So the Scottish Queen and her Catholic friends became more and more suspect of plotting against Elizabeth, who was urged to sign Mary's death warrant.

But Elizabeth could remember all too clearly how, when she was a child, she learned that her mother, Anne Boleyn, had been beheaded on the orders of her father, Henry Vlll; and the terror she had felt when, as a prisoner in the Tower of London, her own life was in similar danger. So, although there were times when she toyed with the idea of having Mary secretly poisoned, she could not bring herself to sign a warrant for the execution of her cousin.

**"My scaffolde was the bedde where ease I founde."**

In 1587 Mary was at last found guilty, in spite of her protests of innocence, of being associated with the Babington Plot to murder Elizabeth. After hesitating for six months, Elizabeth finally signed the death-warrant, and Mary was beheaded, at the age of forty-four, in Fotheringhay Castle in Northamptonshire.

The execution took place on a wooden stage set in the middle of the hall of the Castle. Mary was led in, wearing a black satin gown and long white veil. Her ladies, Elizabeth Curle and faithful old Jane Kennedy, removed the veil and gown, leaving a red velvet petticoat. After she had spent some time in prayer, Mary was blindfolded and made to kneel down at the execution block. She cried out three or four times:

> *"In manus tuas, Domine, commendo spiritum meum."*
> ( *"Into Thy hands, O Lord, I commend my spirit."*)

The chief executioner, whose name was Bulle, struck down with his heavy axe, but did not completely sever the head from the body. The second stroke completed the deed, and Bulle bent down to pick up the head by the hair. There was a gasp of horror from the people in the hall when the auburn wig that Mary had been wearing over her own short, grey hair, came away in his hand and her bare head fell to the floor.

Next, Bulle began to search for Mary's garters which he was allowed to keep as a memento of his deed. As he did so, Mary's little pet dog, a Skye terrier, crept from under her long skirt to cower between the shoulders and the severed head. The dog would not move until Mary's body was taken away, and afterwards it refused to eat and pined away.

"Alive a Queen, now dead I am a Saint."

The execution block was burned immediately, and all Mary's clothes and other belongings which she had not mentioned in her will were destroyed, so that they could not be preserved as relics of a martyr.

The body was placed in a very heavy lead coffin, which was unburied for some months, until it was placed in a vault in Peterborough Cathedral. ( Fotheringhay Castle later became a ruin, and has now completely disappeared.)

In 1603 Mary's son united the two thrones when he became King James 1 of Great Britain. He appears to have shown little love for the mother whom he had never really known, or even grief at her death. But now he gave orders for her body to be brought to London, where it was buried in Westminster Abbey in a magnificent tomb covered by a full-length effigy in white marble. This portrays the real nobility and beauty of Mary's face, and in a tranquility which she had seldom known during her tempestuous career.

For four hundred years, Mary Stuart has been the subject of innumerable books, plays, songs and poems, and there have been heated arguments about her role in history. Thus her motto has been justified:

" IN MY END IS MY BEGINNING "

READING LIST

| | | |
|---|---|---|
| 1811 | Prof. W. Robertson | : "The History of Scotland Under the Reigns of Mary and James Vl" |
| 1831 | Sir Walter Scott | : "The Abbot" (esp. historical notes) |
| 1854 | Agnes Strickland | : "Lives of the Queens of Scotland" |
| 1864 | P. F. Tytler | : "History of Scotland"  (Vols. 1V to Vlll ) |
| 1901 | Robert Burns-Begg | : "The Secrets of My Prison House" |
| 1905 | Sir J.Balfour Paul | : "The Scots Peerage" (Editor) |
| n/d | David Masson | : Articles in "The Perth Collection"  (11,12)  Sandeman Library |
| 1965 | G.Donaldson | : "Edinburgh History of Scotland"  (Vol. 3 )  Oliver & Boyd |
| 1967 | ditto | : "Scottish Kings"  Batsford |
| 1970 | ditto(Editor) | : "Scottish Historical Documents"  Scottish Academic Press |
| 1969 | Lady Antonia Fraser | : "Mary Queen of Scots"  Weidenfeld & Nicolson |
| 1981 | ditto | : Anthology of Poems  Eyre Methuen |
| 1974 | Madelaine Bingham | : "Mary Queen of Scots"  Allen & Unwin |
| 1982 | R.Strong & J.T.Oman | : "Mary Queen of Scots"  Secker & Warburg |

Pamphlet : "Lochleven Castle"            Department of the Environment

*Irene Aitken*

....no more the glance
Of blazing tapers through its window beams
And quivers on the undulating waves;
But naked stand the melancholy walls.......
　　　　　　　　　Michael Bruce